CORNISH REFLECTIONS

JILLY CARTER

BOSSINEY BOOKS

First published in 1988 by
Bossiney Books
St Teath, Bodmin, Cornwall.

Typeset and Printed by
Clowes Book Printers
St Columb, Cornwall.

ISBN 0 948158 45 X

Front cover: Old Fishermen
at Newlyn.

Back Cover: Falmouth Docks.

PLATE ACKNOWLEDGMENTS
The Author and Publisher are most grateful to all the following
people who have kindly loaned their old photographs: Ben Batten,
George Bishop, Ray Bishop, Major Bolitho, Richard Carew Pole,
Suzanne Carter, Marjorie Deacon, EEC International,
Mildred Gape, Peter Gilson and Falmouth Polytechnic Society,
Glasney Press, Myrtle Jones, Kay Larsen, Launceston Museum,
George Maddever, Freddie May, Eddie Murt, The National Trust,
the late Frank Nute and Ivan Nute, A. J. Pengelly, Jim Richardson,
Mrs Rowling, Saltash Heritage Collection, Roy Shambrook, Bill
Taylor, TSW Library, Mrs Uglow, Steve Veal and William
Woolcock.

About the Author and the Book

Jilly Carter is one of the best known characters in Westcountry television.

Born at Widnes, Cheshire, in 1953 and educated at Huyton College near Liverpool, she acquired a BA London degree in English, French and History of Art. She then went to Paris, teaching and modelling Spring collections for various Paris fashion houses. Later she moved to Lisbon for more teaching — and later still went on to Rome. In Rome she did more teaching, helped to research an historical travel book on Darius the Great, read the news on an American radio station and presented the Girl Friday Show.

Jilly Carter came back to do Radio 4 presentation, before moving to Bournemouth where she became a disc jockey-presenter on a live daily show. It was television that brought her to the Westcountry, when in 1982 she joined Television South West. She began at Plymouth working with Gus Honeybun as a continuity announcer and was then promoted to the Newsroom as a presenter and reporter on the nightly 'Today' programme. Since then she has worked on a variety of programmes including 'The Business Show'. She also had the distinction of presenting live satellites with a station in North Carolina to celebrate their 400th

The Author at Trethevy Quoit.

anniversary.

She now lives with her young daughter Lizzie in South Devon, after spending several years at Crow's Nest, high on the edge of Bodmin Moor. It was there that she came to know and love Cornwall. Her interests include antiques collecting, the theatre, cooking, riding and travel. This is her first book, and she is currently researching a second title for Bossiney.

In *Cornish Reflections,* Jilly

Carter thoughtfully, perceptively, combines text and old photographs, many coming from private family collections and appearing in book form for the first time. 'This, then,' she reflects, 'is a personal journey through Cornwall, woven with memories and anecdotes of the many people who've lent me their precious photographs.'

Cornish Reflections is a valuable addition to the Westcountry library — and for all who love Cornwall.

Cornish Reflections

'As a body of men, they are industrious and intelligent, sober and orderly, neither soured by hard work, nor easily depressed by harsher privations . . . I never met so few grumblers anywhere.'

That's how the Victorian author Wilkie Collins described the Cornish when he was touring Cornwall in the 1880s. Grumblers they may not have been, but over the centuries, they had much to endure. They were an isolated community, who had to carve out a tough living on a harsh Atlantic coast, and on barren moorland. They had to dig deep for the wealth that lay buried beneath their feet, and thousands lost their lives in the process. The seas were harsh and rough, and did not give up their catch easily.

It's no wonder then, that for all those centuries, the Cornish were considered — and liked to be considered — a race apart. They were the last area in Britain to be invaded by the Romans. They preserved their political independence for longer than any other part of Britain. They

LEFT & BELOW *'The Cornish like to be considered a race apart.' Two Cornish generations earlier this century.*

were renowned as a resilient, conservative nation, slow to change and tenacious to the past. Many believed that when the West stood up for Charles I during the Civil War, it was Cornwall's immortal hour. For when a Parliamentary force under Lord Stamford came upon Launceston, the Cornish rallied round a destitute Sir Beville Grenville, scaled Stratton Hill, and drove Stamford back to Exeter, with a loss of two thousand men. The King wrote a letter of thanks to the Cornish in 1643, and that letter still hangs in Cornish churches to this day.

Cornwall is justifiably proud of the famous people it's produced. It was at Redruth that William Murdock lit the first house with gas; it was at Illogan that Richard Trevithick invented the steam engine. The first wireless message was sent across the Atlantic by Marconi from the Lizard, and it was at Penzance that Sir Humphry Davy, who invented the safety lamp, was born.

The western end of Cornwall, places like Newlyn, Lamorna and St Ives have drawn painters like a magnet. The prestige of the Newlyn School in the art world today speaks volumes for Cornwall's ability to fire creativity. Cornwall has produced outstanding native painters too: John Opie in the eighteenth century and more recently Peter Lanyon to name just two. Internationally famous characters, like the potter Bernard Leach and the sculptor Dame Barbara Hepworth, significantly chose to make Cornwall their home.

BELOW *A woman's work and a man's work, beautifully illustrated here on St Ives beach, at the turn of the century, or even a little earlier. While the women hang out their washing to dry, the men prepare for their journey out to sea.*

BELOW *The 'Charlotte' — a Westcountry trading ketch, beached at St Ives, around 1890. Her load of coal from South Wales is being taken off in the time-honoured and time-consuming way: by horse and cart.*

Writers, too, have found inspiration here. Arguably more has been written and painted, potted and sculpted in Cornwall than anywhere else in Britain outside London.

Cornwall and the Cornish is a rich and fascinating subject. This particular book looks at the lives of the Victorian and Edwardian Cornish man and woman, at work and at leisure, at war and at peace, through a series of rare photographs. It captures a Cornwall which has, for the most part, long disappeared.

The camera is always a sensitive instrument. In one mood it can be suspicious and probing; in another, it can be historic, capturing all from the momentous to the mundane. In these pages, a whole generation of people have captured Cornish reflections. Some photographs saw the light of publication inside books and newspapers, others were destined for the family album.

The period under the camera's lens is one of upheaval. The fishing and mining industries were to see changes which would completely alter the working lives of generations. With the coming of the railways and development of the waterways, Cornwall was no longer a 'dark', inaccessible place. Visitors began to arrive, attitudes started to alter. Omnibuses and cars would soon shatter the quiet calm of the winding lanes. The loosening of attitudes towards drinking and religion would undo much of John Wesley's work and weaken his considerable influence.

This, then, is a personal journey through Cornwall, woven with memories and anecdotes from the many people who've lent me their precious photographs. I hope it brings as much pleasure to those who read it as it has to me compiling it.

My grateful thanks go to my two year-old daughter Lizzie, who showed great patience, strapped in the back of my car for hours on end, during my search for more photographs and more memories up and down Cornwall.

LEFT *An old fisherman pauses to reflect on times gone by, as he gazes out over Newlyn harbour. He's standing in Fore Street, known locally as 'the Narrows'. Many of these houses have been pulled down, but Ben Batten, who's lived in the village for many years, remembers when he used to ride on a bus down these streets, and the bus obscured all light. He also remembers a strange man who lived there, called Arizona Cocobelli. All the children used to be afraid of him, and nobody can say how he got his most bizarre name.*

BELOW *This splendid vehicle, a Wolseley-Siddeley top deck Great Western Railway bus, did the Falmouth-Redruth-Portreath route, from 1907. H. Opie and Sons certainly had an up-front image, and made sure their name was one of the first to be advertised on the new service.*

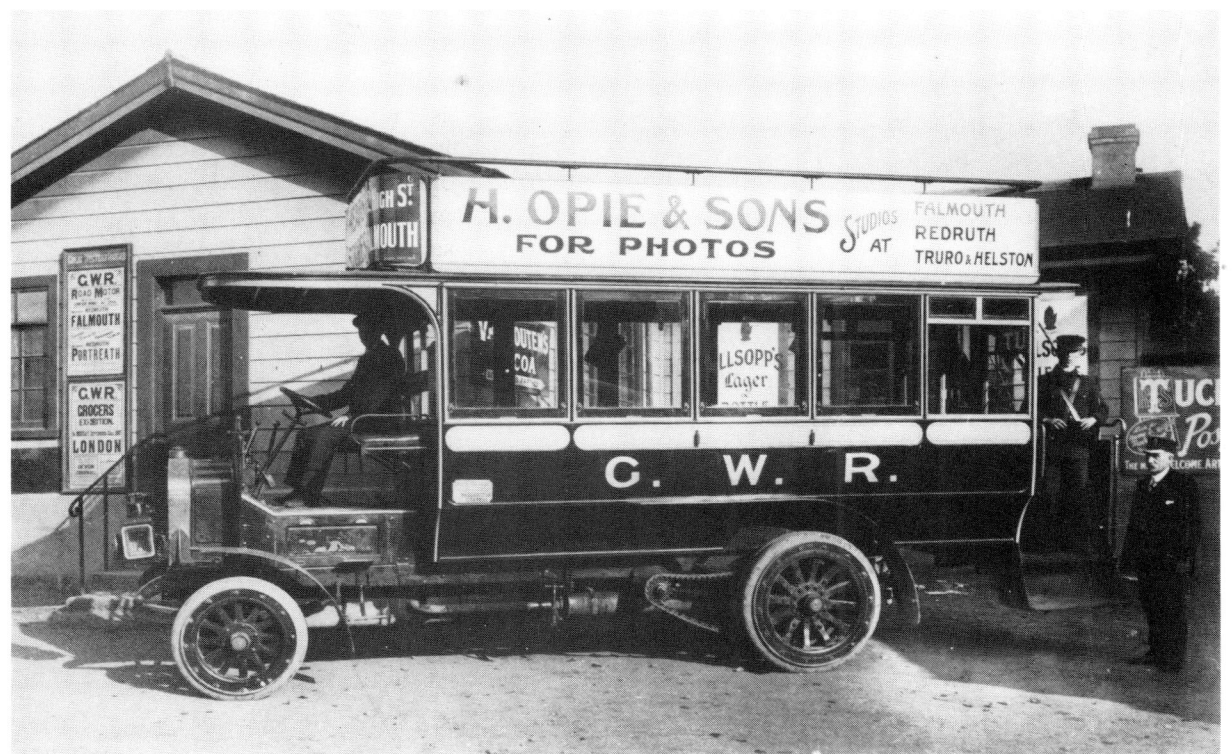

SALTASH

BELOW The building of the Royal Albert Bridge, seen from the Saltash side of the River Tamar. This is the point at which our journey through this land — and it is a land apart — begins. The idea of the bridge first became a reality when the Cornwall Railway Company received its Act of Parliament in 1846, granting it the right to construct a line from Plymouth to Falmouth — a distance of 65.5 miles.

Its architect, Isambard Kingdom Brunel, first thought of constructing a steam train ferry from Saltash Passage, on the Devon side, to Saltash in Cornwall. It would have been 1,000 feet in length. But under the Act, the Cornwall Railway Company was only allowed to cross the Tamar by means of a bridge. Many projects were examined and discarded before Brunel finally came up with the present solution. They included a bridge of Baltic pine, and the extravagant idea of a single span bridge of 850 feet, weighing 7,000 tons, and costing half a million pounds. A tidy

LEFT *The portly and impressive figure of Isambard Kingdom Brunel, a man who did much for Cornwall, seen here second from the right at the launching of the 'Great Eastern'. He was born in Portsmouth in 1806, and from an early age, showed great drive and determination to make something of himself. It was he who helped to plan the Thames tunnel, and took on the construction of the Clifton Suspension Bridge in 1829. Brunel was the designer of the 'Great Western' — the first steamship built to cross the Atlantic, and the 'Great Eastern', then the largest vessel ever built, was constructed under his sole direction from 1852-8. With such a track record behind him, it wasn't surprising he was appointed engineer to the Great Western Railway. He was at the helm to build all the tunnels, bridges and viaducts of that line. Cornwall's famous debt to him is of course the Royal Albert Bridge, which finally exhausted him. He died shortly after it was opened.*

sum in 1846! But in 1848, the Admiralty finally approved a two-span bridge, each span of 450 feet, with seventeen land spans. There was to be a headway of 100 feet above the water.

So Brunel began his exploration of the Tamar river bed, which was dense with oysters. He worked out a process for doing this by using a wrought iron cylinder, floated out in two halves, bolted together mid-stream, and borings made down to the river below.

After a four year delay, work on the bridge resumed in 1852, and it was finally opened, all 2,000 feet of it, on the second of May 1859. The Prince Consort, Prince Albert had given his permission for the bridge to be named after him, and it was he who performed the opening ceremony. He did not, however, leave the comfort of his carriage for the royal platform, but gave his address from the carriage steps. He did deign to walk over the bridge later, and was most impressed with what he saw. The spectacular panorama has continued to impress millions of visitors to Cornwall ever since.

BELOW The town of Millbrook became famous in the eighteenth
century for its excellent fishing fleet. Watermen's boats used to
transport villagers to Mutton Cove, on the Devonport side, but
this was the only service; it was erratic, and the boatmen charged
ridiculous prices, knowing they had a captive market. The Earl of
Mount Edgcumbe, who'd already started his own Cremyll Ferry in
about 1884, offered to help out the villagers of Millbrook by
granting landing rights at Cremyll on Mondays only. Within three
years, John Parsons, a local mill owner, started up a thriving ferry
service, using three steamers. Excursions up and down the river
became very popular, and Parsons did very well for himself. He
then sold out to William Gilbert, who founded the Saltash, Three
Towns and District Steamboat Company. Parsons went on to form
another company — the Millbrook Steamboat Company. This
photo, showing the last boat home from Millbrook, was taken
between 1910-1916.

ABOVE The Saltash ferry route was known as the Ash-Torre
Passage, and it was owned by the de Valletorts, unitl it was sold
to Richard, Earl of Cornwall in 1270. Ferry rights were granted to
the Mayor and Burgess of Saltash by royal grant in 1337, and were
valid for 200 years. It was a steam-operated ferry, until it closed in
October 1961. One of the last ferrymen, Gerald Truscott, recalls
the hard work it took to run the ferry. His working day began at
four in the morning, rowing out to the ferry and bringing her
ashore. Work on the Saltash side started, with filling tanks being
loaded with five hundred gallons of fresh water. Hoses were made
of canvas, and often split, adding to the work-load. The ferry was
taken over to the St Budeaux side of the river, where two to three
tons of coal were loaded — by shovel and wheelbarrow! The ferry
was then taken mid-stream, the donkey engines started up, the
hoses unreeled and the ferry hosed down with salt water. Then it
was back to Saltash, to polish all the copper and brass.
The first ferry left at six in the morning, with extra ferries on
Sunday for the market gardeners from Liskeard, Callington and
the Tamar valley, so they could get their produce to Plymouth
market. The last ferry left at eleven at night, and, except for
mishaps such as groundings, always left on time.

BELOW Locals stop for a tasty snack at Mary Ann Pope's cockle shop in Tamar Street, Saltash, known for centuries to sailors as Picklecockle Alley. On offer, whelks, oysters, crabs and shrimps caught fresh from the Tamar. Mary Ann's shop was the forerunner of the Wimpy bar, and she turned her living room to great commercial advantage, making quite a tidy sum for her wares. Note the charming floral wallpaper!

ABOVE An unrecognisable, and highly decorated Saltash Fore Street. As the new Saltash by-pass, with its huge tunnel cutting a swathe around the town nears completion, it's sad to look at this photograph and see how much has gone for ever. It probably depicts the festivities after the Coronation of King George V on 22 June 1911, as W. H. Smith's, on the right, opened somewhere around 1910. The whole of the left hand side of Fore Street was destroyed in the Blitz in 1941, as was the lovely Tudor first-floor building on the right. And what Hitler's bombs didn't manage to obliterate, modern town planning in the early sixties certainly did.

ABOVE This postcard – a collector's item from the studios of
Harris in Quethiock – shows two women limpet-pickers, wrapped
up against the winter in the shelter of a cave at Downderry. Who
knows, they could well be the famous Irish widows who lived in a
cave outside the village for thirty years. When the weather became
too inclement, they went to sleep in a disused pigsty. Despite local
efforts to send them to the workhouse, they managed to remain
independent to the end. Poor they may have been, but they were
fiercely proud. They were quoted as saying, 'Never, sir, will us go
to the workhouse when us can get as much as one crust in twenty
four hours.'

ANTONY

BELOW Anyone for tennis? Members of the Carew Pole family from Antony House at Torpoint, knock up a few balls on the family lawn court. It must have been hot and sticky work, dressed in full Edwardian attire, and we can see the gentlemen didn't even remove their hats. This is a good view of the north front and terrace of the house, which was built in the early eighteenth century, and given to the National Trust in 1961 by Sir John Carew Pole.

LEFT A prosperous corn merchant by the name of James Carne takes time out of his busy day to pose for this photograph in 1905, at Beales Mill, near the Duchy of Cornwall headquarters at Stoke Climsland. He's joined by his wife Jane Anne and young son Sidney. The water mill is now used by a cattle feed merchant.

Calstock railway viaduct. In 1904 the Plymouth, Devonport and South Western Junction Railway began work on linking up their station at Bere Alston, with the East Cornwall Mineral Railway line from Kelly Bray, near Callington, to Calstock Quay. The whole construction of this majestic viaduct was carefully recorded for posterity by a local photographer, Frederick Paul, who used to sell the photographs as postcards. His daughter Marjorie appears as a little girl, with her sister, in much of his work around the village. She's very much alive and well, and still living in Calstock. Passengers going up and down the river on the regular paddle-steam service must have been greatly impressed by the construction of this twelve-arched edifice, and they must have really felt part of the tremendous industrial revolution they were living through. There was such an enormous amount of industrial activity going on in the early nineteenth century, that good communications became not only desirable, but absolutely essential. A canal network had already been set up throughout the country, roads were beginning to improve, and the world's first public railway opened in 1825, between Stockton and Darlington. The 1820s also saw the rise of the steam ship, used as tugs, coastal packets and passenger ferries. The Tamar, with all its tributaries and creeks, was one of the busiest rivers in the area, and with the boom in mining, quarrying and agriculture, all sorts of boats were working to the limit, loading and unloading goods.

Around this period, passenger and market steamers were being used on the Tamar, to ports like Calstock, Millbrook, Torpoint, Saltash, Cotehele and Morwellham. Day trips up the river became the 'Thing to Do', and of course people dressed up for the occasion. As Alan Kettridge notes in his book *Passenger Steamers of the River Tamar,* by the turn of the century, the Tamar valley had the largest collection of esturial paddle steamers on the south coast of England.

ABOVE Clitters Mine, near Gunnislake, which produced large quantities of arsenic. On the hill to the left is the mine captain's house. To the right, the River Tamar gently wends its way through the woodland. The belching stack is an arsenic flue; many still run underground like a labyrinth, through Albaston village. Arsenic was used in the clarification of glass, and some was exported to the United States, where it was used in making pesticides to combat bugs in the cotton plants. It's interesting to note how much foreign investment there was in smaller mines in the Gunnislake area in the late 1890s. The Norwegian Exploration Company held shares in the mine setts of Clitters, Hawkmoor and Hingston Down consols, which were all working as one mine. £160,000 was raised to work and develop these mines for tin, wolfram and arsenic. Over 100 men were employed here. *Venning's Postal Directory* notes that by the turn of the century, the Prince of Wales Mine at Harrowbarrow had Frenchmen as its shareholders, with a head office in Paris!

BELOW Shareholders at Wheal Arthur, near Calstock, about to go down in to the cage to inspect the levels. The mine was only worked down to the deep adit — a depth of some 50 fathoms. Old workings went down 300 feet under that. The mine produced some tin and wolfram. In this photogrpah, taken in 1919, we see Alfred Doidge, standing up top. With his long beard and sideboards, he used to like being addressed as 'Captain'.

ABOVE When things began to turn sour for the miners in the early twenties, those who chose to stay in Cornwall were forced to re-think their job situation, and try their hand at whatever could earn them a crust. For many, fruit-picking seemed a reasonable option. Waste ground was taken over, and turned into allotments on which suitable produce could be cultivated. 'Sheba Bottoms' in Stoke Climsland was one such scheme, named after the mine Wheal Sheba. It used land adjacent to the mine, and gave a couple of generations of miners a profitable existence. But they were always at the mercy of cheaper imported goods or fruit from more favoured areas like St Dominick, where production was more professional and more intense. It looks somehow rather incongruous to see hardened old miners, familiar with the vicissitudes of life underground, handling such delicate fruit as strawberries, in the heat of the summer sun.

BELOW The carriage awaits for Sir Frederick Wills, who fought two Parliamentary elections here at Launceston, in 1895 and 1898. The White Hart, which gave its name to this famous Launceston hotel, stands draped in bunting and flags. It was from this elegant hotel that the wealthy ordered their post chaises, and from which the mail coach left. Taking four passengers inside, and four outside, it reached Exeter in six or seven hours. A daily coach from Exeter to Falmouth took an excruciating fourteen hours. It was called the 'Regulator', and carried sixteen weary passengers.

The White Hart prided itself on its cuisine, and menus from the turn of the century reveal that a double bedroom would cost four shillings, with a ham, eggs and steak breakfast thrown in at two shillings and sixpence. Fire and lights were one and sixpence extra per day, and for a cold bath — perish the thought — the price was sixpence.

ABOVE LEFT During both World Wars, Launceston Town Hall was used as a hospital for wounded soldiers. Here a group of solemn and dedicated Red Cross nurses show their devotion to duty in a formal pose for the camera, round 1918.

LEFT The Old Butter Market in Launceston Square now replaced by the war memorial.

ABOVE The men and boys that made up R. Worth Coach Builders of Launceston, in front of their premises at the turn of the century. The Castle Stores wagon — advertising themselves as tiptop grocers — is parked in front. That shop is now a high class fruit and vegetable store.

BELOW Prockter's Cycle Show, held in the Western Rooms, Launceston in 1899. These rooms are now occupied by the *Cornish and Devon Post*. The bicycles must have made a very fine spectacle, with all the latest models on view. People came from miles around to visit the show, and brought good business to the town. Launceston was a thriving place at the turn of the century, with many profitable industries. Almost every cottage had a spinning wheel, and a yarn market was held every Wednesday. It was so successful that seven spinning mills were set up, one of which employed two hundred people. There were also wool staplers and fellmongers, and there were eight tanyards and tucking mills for making serge, which had worked for two centuries powered by waterwheels. Thirty men worked as hat-makers, there were twenty one boot-makers, five basket-makers, four saddlers, four tinsmiths and eight blacksmiths. There were also nine bakehouses, as very few of the working class had cooking grates. They made their bread at home, then took it to the bakehouse to bake it.

ABOVE A group of Victorian gentry, caught in a moment of leisure at elegant Stourscombe House, Launceston. Croquet was very popular at the time, but it was of course de rigeur to keep your hat on. The first reference to this lovely house was in the rent rolls of the borough in 1512, when it appears to have been set apart from the lands called 'Barnham', and charged with the annual rent of '1lb of pepper'. In 1572, when John Wyse was the tenant of Stourscombe, there's an entry in the borough steward's roll of the payment 'of 4d for an ounce of pepper that lacked of John Wyse's rent'. There were 83 tenants of borough land in 1578, the total rental being £74. 8s $4\frac{1}{2}$d and 1 lb of pepper', the pepper being charged to John Wyse, 'for the high rent of Sturscombe'. The house was sold in 1875 to a Mr Moore of Badcock and Moore for £1,205, after the death of its owner Colonel Cotgrave of the Royal Navy.

ABOVE Legend has it that nowhere else in Cornwall does the sea rise so high as in Bude, and that rolling, crashing sea can be heard as far as ten miles away. It's known as a notoriously difficult place to photograph, because of its spaciousness, and it was seen as a challenge for the Victorian mining engineer Herbert Hughes, whose work is seen elsewhere in this book. Here, at the breakwater, a solitary fishing boat is moored in harbour, and two women take the air on a cool spring afternoon.

Two old Boscastle street scenes.

RIGHT It seems rather incongruous that a custard king should become the champion of so noble a figure as King Arthur. But it was indeed a certain Mr Frederick Glasscock, of Monk and Glass Custard Powders, London, who helped to transform the shadowy king's birthplace into an enormous tourist attraction. Glasscock visited Tintagel while he was on holiday in Cornwall during the First World War. He fell in love with the place, and decided to make his home there. While a luxury bungalow was being built for him, he had plenty of time on his hands to study all that was known of Arthur and his knights. When his home was completed in 1919 — with its nine bedrooms, tennis courts and bowling green — Glasscock had become totally immersed in his hero.

BELOW Hall of Chivalry and King Arthur's Hall. Glasscock then turned his attention to Trevena House, the holiday home of Sir Arthur and Lady Hayter, which he saw as the perfect place to re-create King Arthur's Hall. He acquired it in 1927, and work began at once, using various types of Cornish stone. Glasscock wanted the whole thing to be a local affair; all the materials were local, and so was the workforce. There was great excitement as the opening approached in 1933. For here, a labour of dedication and

When Frederick Glasscock died in 1934, following a successful recruiting programme in the United States, he was much mourned. His wife returned to their bungalow, which was called Eirenikon (meaning Peace), but her heart was no longer in the Movement, and the Fellowship could never be the same without his driving force and enthusiasm.

love had been realised: its magnificent stained glass windows, its great hall lit by oak torches, and its enormous Round Table, made for both the Christian and the heathen to sit at. Glasscock's memorial to King Arthur was no empty edifice, however; it was to become a place of great activity. A society, known as the Fellowship of the Round Table, was formed and, as the movement grew, local children were enrolled as Searchers (of the Holy Grail, perhaps?). They then progressed to become Pilgrims, and eventually they could attain the honour of becoming Knights of the Fellowship, and attend monthly investitures.

Glasscock was — to many — Mr Tintagel. Rich he certainly was, but his generosity was as legendary as the King himself. Whenever he heard of a family in need, he'd send logs and coal, with stockings and shoes for the children. Nobody went short at Christmas. There were parties and balls and tea parties at the Hall, which was always a place of elegance — and fun. But the locals did their bit to help Mr Glasscock, when help was needed. During the War, eggs were in short supply, so local fishermen collected sea gulls' eggs, to send to the custard factory in London. So there *was* still custard for tea!

31

RIGHT Trebarwith Strand earlier this century. Note the parked carriages and the one motor car. The Strand was popular with visitors in those days as it is today.

LEFT Photography was all the rage at the turn of the century. And thank goodness that, when it came to photographs, this generation was no throw-away society: they cherished them, and kept them safe in leather-bound albums. And there was a sense of occasion when they were brought out for friends to see. This early photograph, around 1907, was taken by a man who travelled all over Cornwall, snapping local sights of history and natural beauty. His friend stands in the legendary Merlin's cave, at the foot of King Arthur's Castle at Tintagel. The wooden bridge above him was used to take tourists up to the castle for hundreds of years, but it eventually rotted away, and a new one was placed there the easy way: by helicopter.

RIGHT *The Telegraph,* just landed at Castle Cove, Tintagel, in about 1885. She came to take slate from two quarries — Lamb's House and Long Grass — and in return, she brought coal from Cardiff. One of the first cutters was a man called Jimmy Tinney, still remembered by the older residents of the village. On the left of this early photograph is the whimround, the apparatus used to load the slate. The castle is in the background.

There was a great deal of house-building around Tintagel in about 1910, and slate from such quarries as the Prince of Wales Slate Quarry and Lamb's House, owned by the Reverend Kinsman, was used for this purpose.

LEFT Donkey boys, hard at work loading sand onto beasts.

RIGHT Family and employees pose for the cameras outside one of Wadebridge's better-known boot shops in Molesworth Street, around 1912. A wide variety of boots and shoes were on offer in the windows of the double-fronted corner shop, all hand-sewn on the premises. One doubts if there was any fancy sophisticated footwear on sale here; the emphasis was very much on no-nonsense, practical and sturdy shodding. The shop continued selling shoes up until very recently.

LEFT John Cocks was known far and wide for his marvellous
bread, which won him many prizes. This photograph taken
outside his shop in Wadebridge around 1915, shows most of the
Cocks family, with John in baker's dress on the left. His father, a
retired policeman also called John, is the bearded gentleman in
front of the pony and trap, which carried the firm's products to
outlying villages. Travel was never easy at the best of times for
most local people, and the First World War exacerbated the
situation. So Cock's carriages, laden with sweet-smelling bread and
cakes, were a welcome sight in villages such as St Mabyn, Port
Isaac and Delabole. When John Cocks retired, exhausted after so
many 3 a.m. starts, his sisters took over; they're seen standing in
the doorway with their mother. The shop still exists in
Wadebridge today: it's now a grocer's. Locals still refer to this
corner of Wadebridge as Cock's Corner.

RIGHT The marriage of Mr and Mrs Charles George at the
Egloshayle Road United Methodist Church, Wadebridge in 1906.
Obviously a sombre occasion, with not a smile to be seen. Perhaps
that's because all the in-laws were there too, making it a tense
moment for the newly weds, Janice and Charles. The bride was
formerly a Woolcock, a name to be reckoned with still today in
Wadebridge! Harry Woolcock was the driver of the town's Jersey
car, and it's his son William, now in his late seventies, who lent
me this photograph.

LEFT A horse-drawn carriage — a Jersey car to be precise —
outside Wadebridge town hall before 1914. It's a St Breock church
outing, organised by Robert Woolcock, whose carriages made
pleasure trips around Newquay, Boscastle, Tintagel and as far as
Truro. Mr Woolcock is the man in the bowler, checking last
minute details. Included in the party is Miss Minnie Pasco, in her
striped costume, Mrs Hosken, wearing a mourning band on her
arm (her husband used to ride on horseback in front of the annual
Wadebridge carnival) and the bowler-hatted man with the silver
beard, a Mr Miller, a retired police inspector. Almost out of shot is
Molten, a white horse with a will of iron. No hill was too steep for
him, and he had to be unhitched on many an occasion, as he'd
exhaust the other horses, by dragging on to the bitter end. It was
Mr Woolcock who organised the big Royal Marines outing to
Tintagel, as seen in the photograph overleaf.

ABOVE Wadebridge Male Voice Choir, out in force in a smart charabanc, on their way to a performance in the 1920s. Standing on the right, is a dapper Doctor Wilson-Gunn, with a fresh pansy in his buttonhole. A practising GP in the town, he was the choir's conductor, and by all accounts, a hard task-master, who demanded high standards and usually got them. Male voice choirs have always been popular in Cornwall, and there have been many famous ones. Note the postman on the left, trudging up the hill in his stout shoes and now-antiquated cap.

BELOW Make way for the boys! The Royal Marines hit town in 1910 in two horse-drawn vehicles, and caused quite a sensation in the centre of Wadebridge. The men, in high spirits, were on a day's outing to Tintagel, and had just been picked up from the Plymouth train. And everyone in the town wanted a good look at them, especially the ladies. The maids at the Commercial Hotel, now the Swan, opened the windows for a good view. Pity the poor horses, who had an arduous day ahead of them, pulling so many men up so many hills en route to King Arthur's Castle.

RIGHT Treguddick Bridge, Wadebridge, from the site of Brooklyn garage. The Regal cinema has ousted the building behind the hump-back stone bridge, and the Bible Christian chapel has since been turned into the Cosy Cafe on the right. Part of the cafe hires out videos, which now seem to be more in demand in many households than Bibles!

LEFT Sladesbridge, just outside Wadebridge around 1910, and would that it looked now, as it did then. A peaceful, balmy summer's day, with children safely playing in the meadow, and young lads dangling their legs over the edge of the bridge. The fields are full of flowers, there's a lushness and stillness which seem so hard to find these days. Time to stand and stare. The bridge has since been considerably widened to take the heavy traffic which passes through the village, and the cottage up on the right is no longer thatched.

ABOVE Young and old come under the camera's lens for this photograph taken in Padstow's Market Square in 1910. They're all standing in front of Eve and Daisy Sloccett's shop, eyes screwed up against a strong sun. The road sweeper in his dusty clothes and battered hat is probably glad of the rest. All the girls are in their pinafores and hats, and the boy on the far right carries an iron hoop. Rolling hoops, which were controlled by a stick with a shepherd's hook on the end, was a great pastime in villages all over the country at the turn of the century, and the noise of the iron, clattering over cobbled streets, was a familiar sound. It was probably preferable to the noise of today's skateboards! And it was almost always safe to play in the streets, as there were very few, if any cars about. The Misses Sloccetts ran a thriving business in the town, and often allowed customers to put things on the slate. Credit was an accepted practice, and a common phrase to be heard at the time was 'I'll pay you for that in the herring season'. Then the town became prosperous, and there was plenty of cash about. The same applied in the trawling season, when Scottish fishergirls came down to smoke kippers.

44

One can only imagine the intense excitement the unearthing of an ancient British cemetery near Padstow in 1900 must have caused at the time. Everybody was talking about it, and the newspapers were full of the discovery of this piece of the far and distant past at Harlyn Bay. The Iron Age village, with its cists, or graves, dates back to about 500 BC, and brought crowds in their thousands to take a closer look. It all started with the digging of a well, then the first grave was discovered under a sand mound near the sea.

ABOVE The immensely popular tourist town of Newquay — mecca for sun worshippers, beachcombers and surfers. It was once the typical Cornish fishing village, known then just for its pilchard catches. The railway came here in 1875 — later than most of the rest of Cornwall. It was in 1439 that Bishop Lacey of Exeter granted the indulgence for the construction, repair and maintenance of a harbour here. Pilchards soon became plentiful, and the most legendary catch was in 1863, when the largest catch ever known on the north coast of Cornwall was pulled in. The pilchards stretched literally from Trevelgue Head to Towan Head, and the catch was worth £20,000.

RIGHT Sarah's Shaft at Wheal Kitty, near St Agnes, where the beam pumping engine is being dismantled. With his back to the camera is Jack Trouson, who was an expert on mining surveys. In his young days he worked at East Pool, then he became head surveyor at South Crofty. During his retirement, he wrote many excellent books on mining in Cornwall. He died in 1987.

If you see a hole, a deep hole, anywhere in the world, chances are you'll find a Cornishman down it. That's the old saying, and it's a pretty accurate one. Cornwall has always had the richest metals and minerals in Britain, and from earliest times, she knew the value of trading with foreign nations. She began commerce with the Romans in the first century, but the earliest traders for tin with Cornwall were probably the Phoenicians, who, from their colony at Gades on the Western coast of Spain, were the main commercial link between the two countries. Cornish tin was much in demand in the sixth and seventh centuries, when bells were introduced in churches and cathedrals in Western Europe.

King John was the first to grant a charter to the tinners of Cornwall and Devon. And by the time of Richard, Duke of Cornwall, production was considerable. Under charters, given by both King John and King Edward I, tinners were given the right to take turf and wood for smelting their tin, just as in ancient times, and so reduce the ore. Tinners paid a tax to the Earls and Dukes of Cornwall after it was smelted and cast into blocks. Each block was marked with the smelter's stamp, and taken to various towns in Cornwall to make coins. They included Lostwithiel, Truro, Bodmin and Helston. In 1838, these duties were abolished, and compensation in lieu of them was given.

But it wasn't just tin that was there for the taking; there was copper, zinc, wolfram, silver ore, uranium and arsenic. Walter Tregellas notes, in his book on Cornish history, that in 1878 13,746 mine workers were employed. That was just the beginning of the boom.

RIGHT *Miners waiting for the cage to descend into Dolcoath Mine, about 1890.*

LEFT *West Francis Mine in Carn Brae, with its leaning stack caused by subsidence. Part of the South Francis mine can be seen in the background. There were quite a few stacks which leant this way. One at Downgate, near Luckett, is still leaning!*

So what was life like for the working miner in the early 1880s? Hot, hard and dirty. His working day began at 6 a.m., but he usually got up at half past four, as many miners lived some distance from the mine. Breakfast was tea, bread and butter. His wife would then prepare him a 'hoggan' — an unappetising mixture of flour and water baked with no yeast. He'd eat that — or a pasty — at about 11 a.m.. He worked at least 1,800 feet below ground in what can only be described as hazadous conditions. His uniform hardly provided much protection. He wore a thick flannel

BELOW *'Croust Time' at East Pool Mine. An early photograph, with the men still using felt caps. The boys are wearing the white lining, the cap which went under the miner's harder hat. The group is enjoying a pasty, and some smoke tobacco from Cornish clay pipes. Note the candle stuck on the helmet, and the spare candles hung from the jacket.*

shirt, canvas trousers and coat, heavy boots and a skull cap with a specially-hardened felt hat. On this, he stuck a candle, secured with a lump of sticky clay. Spare candles were slung round his neck, or from a button on his coat. He often worked till six at night, then he had the long walk home. Life expectancy was forty years. Consumption was rife. To say life can't have been much fun is an understatement. It's not surprising so many miners squandered their weekly wage on drink. The Methodist movement had an uphill struggle persuading miners of the dangers of drinking, but they did make inroads, as is evident by the numerous chapels in Cornwall.

It's hard to believe that these grim-faced, tough-looking men, who came face-to-face with death every day, could be so superstitious. Whistling underground was a heinous crime, because it was feared evil spirits would be raised. Many miners believed in pixies and witches. Other superstitions included showing money to the new moon to get more money in return, and knowing that if your palm itched, you'd have something given to you shortly. White specks under the thumb nail was good news, but it was bad news if they appeared under the fingers, and disaster would occur when the nail was long enough for the flecks to be cut out. Miners were also strong believers in dreams and the ancient art of dowsing. It's said that many of the principal mines in Cornwall were discovered by such methods.

ABOVE *South Crofty Mine, where East Pool had their dressing floors. From the 1830s, the mine formed the southern part of East Wheal Crofty. The mine was closed down in 1896, when base metal prices were very depressed, but it was re-opened in 1899. It is still a working mine today. Richard Trevithick, the great Cornish engineer and inventor, was born down the road from the South Crofty counting house.*

RIGHT Dolcoath Mine was one of the largest and deepest in Cornwall, with a bottom level of 3,000 feet beneath the surface. Between 1799 and 1920, its output was nine million pounds. This photograph, taken before 1900, shows bal maidens at the New East Shaft of the mine. It was their job to pick out the copper and arsenic from the stones the men had broken down, And for all this hard labour they were paid six pence a day.

There was, though, a great deal of prejudice regarding the employment of women at all, at this time. George Henwood, writing in the 1850s leaves us in no doubt as to his opinion on the matter: 'The indiscriminate association, in their employment, of the sexes naturally begets a want of modesty and delicacy, so important in the formation of the female character; whilst the masculine labour which females are frequently compelled to undertake, together with them being so long from home, render them wholly unfit to perform and attend to those domestic duties which should constitute the comfort and charm of every home, particularly that of the working man.'

BELOW RIGHT This huge traction engine, driving on the main road from Hayle Docks, must have caused quite a lot of congestion at the time. It's delivering coal from Swansea or Cardiff to the local mines.

RIGHT This is the youngest photograph in the book, taken around 1950. What a shock the inhabitants of this house must have had in the dead of one summer's night. The Hancocks, who lived in this house, knew that they were on the edge of the old Holmbush copper mine, near Downgate. And they had noticed some funny ochre-coloured water bubbling up outside the house. But nothing could prepare them for the rumblings and subsequent collapse of the family home down the mine's shaft. Here, an agent for the local coal yard surveys the damage with his brother. Fortunately, nobody was hurt in the incident, as the whole family managed to get out in time.

LEFT Another photograph of Dolcoath mine. It's October 1896, and the men are measuring the ground to sink Williams' shaft, one of the deepest in Cornwall. It was completed in 1910. Here the men pose before the camera, as the first turf is about to be cut. They obviously all had a sense of occasion on this day; all the young boys are wearing white collars, and the miners are in Sunday best. In the background, is the 'red river' valley to the right of the chimney stacks. All the mining waste seeped its way into the Atlantic, off Cornwall, and it's said that you could see red patches of water up to half a mile out to sea, if you stood up on the cliffs.

ABOVE Wheal Grenville Mine, Camborne, taken around 1900, showing Marshall's Shaft. A good picture of the pumping engine, the balance box and the winding engine. The mine closed down in 1920 — a critical time for the industry. During the First World War, there had been a period of false prosperity. Government pressure for yet more output meant increased production of tin, wolfram and arsenic, which was not in the best interests of sound mining. Only the highest grade ore could be worked, and development of new ore reserves wasn't possible. Tin prices rose to over £400 a ton in 1920, but had dropped back to £141 a ton in 1922. Coal, though, had also gone up from fifteen shillings a ton, to fifty shillings. Mines were then in the unenviable position of either closing down, or getting expensive subsidies to tide them over until reserves were developed.

Cornish miners did their bit in the First World War, although they didn't get the help the coal miners received. But the coal miners had to strike to get what they wanted. The tin miner would not resort to such tactics. And he was to pay the price of such pride. The poverty that existed during the slump was awful, because it wasn't just the mines, but all the other industries dependent on mining, which suffered too. There were the workers in the tin streams, the smelting works, the foundries and the explosives manufacturers. The town of Camborne was so badly affected, that there was no money to light the streets at night. Soup kitchens were set up, and Cornish miners toured the country trying to raise funds for their stricken colleagues. Many miners looked to South Africa and America in their quest for work. It wasn't until 1932 that the price of tin rose again, and the price of materials began to fall. Only then could mining once more become a viable proposition. How ironic that once again the tin industry is in serious trouble in Cornwall, with many mines being forced to shut down — some perhaps never to re-open.

BELOW An early photo of Mitchell's shaft at East Pool mine near Redruth, showing the early timber head gear. To the right, is the Cornish beam engine house, and an unusual steel stack. Behind that is the count house, where all the mining business was transacted. To the left, the ore has just been hoisted up the shaft, and it's being trammed from there by a worker to the processing area. The winding engine is still preserved by the Cornish Engine Preservation Group, and is now in the hands of the National Trust.

ABOVE After the railway reached Cornwall, the first 'connecting services', to places not on the railway, were run by the railways themselves. Here the Great Western pulls out all the stops with a Milnes-Daimler open wagonette, which has stopped for passengers outside Redruth station. The Redruth-Falmouth service was launched in 1907, the date of this photograph. Note the steam rail car in the background. The vehicle caused quite a stir among the locals, as everyone pressed forward for a better look — and to get themselves in the camera's eye.

ABOVE John Wesley maintained that 30,000 men and women of sound Methodist faith could fill this natural amphitheatre of grass and stone. There was obviously a good turn-out for this annual meeting of the faithful towards the turn of the century. Wesley called Gwennap Pit the 'finest amphitheatre in the kingdom', and for him it was the ideal place to preach and teach. The atmosphere that he generated in the 1770s and 1780s lives on; a service is still held here every Whit Monday.

BELOW A tram, full of passengers, makes its way down Wesley Street, Camborne, passing the Weslyan church on the right. The postcard bears an intriguing message on the back: 'Dear Ethel, I hope to see you on Thursday. I have had "some" time. Love from your loving friend Lily.' One can only imagine what Lily got up to in Camborne in November 1924, but she obviously enjoyed herself.

BELOW A scene that will gladden the eyes of older St Ives fishermen — this is how Porthminster Beach used to look at the height of the flourishing fishing industry at the turn of the century. Sailing companies used to keep their seine boats here during the season. Now they're long gone, giving way to deck chairs, ice-cream vendors and bodies bared to the sun.

ABOVE A beautifully dramatic picture of the St Ives fishing fleet, preparing for the coming mackerel season. The boats have spent the winter months laid up at Lelant, and Hayle can just be seen in the distance. These luggers would have embarked on a journey of some 500 miles, fishing in the North Sea or in Ireland, in their search for herring. One can only imagine the hardship the 40 foot boats had to endure for long stretches of time, so far from their families.

RIGHT Barefoot in the street. Mrs Alfred Wallis, wife of the scrap metal dealer-cum-painter, peers down Laity Hill, as a young boy trudges up to Back Road East. He's probably been to the harbour to collect water in his pitcher, as there was no mains water at this time. The little girl on the steps, resting beside a sleeping cat, is Mrs Loveday Stevens, a gracious lady who was in her nineties at the time of writing.

When Mrs Wallis died, her husband Alfred started to paint, when he wasn't collecting iron bedsteads and fireplaces, as seen at the foot of the steps beside his house. He was later to be 'discovered', and his work is now very much sought-after. What a pity for Eddie Murt, the man who loaned me this picture. Poor Eddie used to be given Alfred's pictures for nothing. He threw them away, thinking they were worthless.

BELOW A rare photo, taken around 1880, of the road leading to Porthmeor beach, near St Ives. Porthmeor means 'great cove' in Cornish. The young women have probably just come from Barnoon field, on the left of the photograph, and they're carrying a flasket of clothes — the local word for basket. The women used to dry their weekly wash in the fields, or on the beach, using the round, blue pebbles indigenous to the area, to hold down the corners.

BELOW A certain G. Brown chose this postcard to relay his grocery list to the local shop. On the back, it reads: 'Will you please keep until called for, one pound of best fresh butter, Friday's bread and Saturday's and oblige.' Mrs Carbines, the shopkeeper, no doubt did oblige. With no telephone, the postcard was an invaluable way of sending messages. The post seemed miraculously frequent in the last century, so despite their lack of sophisticated machinery, people did manage to stay in touch.

Picture postcards began in 1869, when a certain Dr Herman from Germany, persuaded his Government to produce a card the size of an envelope, with writing space to contain not more than twenty words. Pictures and advertising followed in 1881, with privately-printed material appearing in 1884. Britain was quick to catch on. The first picture postcards appeared in 1870, designed and printed by Messrs de la Rue. They could only be bought at the Post Office, and cost a halfpenny stamp to send. There was no such thing as an envelope, so the postcard brought communication within the financial reach of everybody. After all, most people could stretch themselves to a penny stamp, if they wanted to let their family know they'd reached their destination safely.

Collecting picture postcards reached cult proportions during Queen Victoria's reign. The Queen herself had a small collection, and she shared her nation's love of putting them in scrap books to show the children and grandchildren.

ABOVE It's best bib and tucker for this jolly party, on their way to the top of Wrovas Hill for the Knill Festival. John Knill was born in Callington in 1734, and he became Mayor of St Ives in 1776. His monument, a granite obelisk, is a perfect landmark for ships at sea. But it's quite a climb for this party, on a warm summer's afternoon in heavy Victorian dress. The festival takes place every five years, on St James's Day. Ten little girls, dressed in white, accompanied by two elderly widows and a fiddler, lead the procession, and once at the top, the children dance round the pyramid-shaped monument, to the tune of the Cornish Furry Dance. After fifteen minutes, they then sing the metric version of the Hundredth Psalm. In this picture, taken around 1910, there's a sad fate in store for the lady in the striped straw hat. She's Mrs Barber, whose son William was to die in the St Ives lifeboat disaster of 1939, when six of the seven crew lost their lives.

LEFT *Two St Ives ladies, mending nets at a hut near the beach around 1890. Many women made a small income out of taking nets into their homes, on a contract basis, or they'd spend their day making sure their husband's nets were in tip-top condition. It was very much a partnership; men and women worked side by side, sharing the load in the struggle to make what could often be an uncertain living out of a cruel sea.*

LEFT A bustling St Ives harbour, in the middle of the winter herring season. Boxes with four handles, called gurries, were taken down to the boat's side, and filled with fish. They were then carried to the women waiting to count them into barrels, to be taken to the fish merchants' cellars. Gurries were probably unique to St Ives, and each one contained about eight hundred herring.

BELOW Tucking pilchards. But of course St Ives wasn't just famous for its herring. On 17 October 1851 the Hope seine, owned by the Ebenezer Fishing Company, took 17,908,800 pilchards, loaded into 5,600 hogs' heads, and sold at 45 shillings a hogs' head.

ABOVE The *Susan Elizabeth* was just one of Cornwall's many famous shipwrecks. She was a schooner, caught in a north east gale at Porthminster, in October 1907. Fortunately, her crew were all rescued by the St Ives lifeboat. The Cornish earned themselves rather a bad reputation when it came to wrecks. Many accused them of being scavangers, but basically, once human life had been saved, a free-for-all was considered fair play. The Cornish attitude was one of grateful acceptance, and they were wont to reflect: 'It's an ill wind that blows no good to Cornwall.' Tinners often made it their business to go to such wrecks, equipped with axes and hatchets. A certain Mr Borlase, wrote with curious detachment about them at the time: 'They'll cut a large trading vessel to pieces in one tide.' When the first lighthouse was constructed on Lizard Point, there was an outcry from the Cornish, because it was considered an action which would deprive people of God's blessing. A nineteenth-century parson, Reverend Troutbeck of the Isles of Scilly, put it rather well, when he said, hedging his and his flock's bets, 'We pray Thee, O Lord, not that wrecks should happen, but that if wrecks do happen, Thou wilt guide them into the Scilly Isles for the benefit of the poor inhabitants.'

BELOW A team to be reckoned with. A group of processors at St Ives pose for a formal photograph. The women have packed the pilchards in the age-old manner, with noses pointing to the side and tails in the centre. Here the man who's standing second on the left holds the stencil for marking the barrels with their destination and brand.

The curing of pilchards was a specialised affair. In Looe, for example, there was a special single-storey building on the sea front called the Albatross, where pilchards were cured in bulk. The fish were taken into an open centre court and piled into heaps. The women then took them into four surrounding buildings and stacked them into miniature hay rick-shaped mounds, with a layer of fish, then a layer of salt, and so on, until they were five feet high. Heavy boards were placed on top of them, then wooden beams, one end of each resting in a hole in the wall of the building, the other end reaching out over the stacked fish, and weighted down with iron weights. The oil was thus extracted, and it ran into small gulleys and down into tanks for collection. The whole curing process took about six weeks.

ABOVE *Children enjoying the seaside at Penzance West Beach, near the reef of rocks between Penzance and Newlyn. To the left is old St Mary's School.*

ABOVE Market Jew Street, Penzance, showing the statue of Humphry Davy, who invented the miners' lamp.

LEFT A solitary pony and trap makes its way down a rather muddy Penzance street, past the Alverton Public buildings at Penzance. Today this is a busy road, linking the town with Land's End and St Just. Impressive wrought iron railings used to grace this building, but, as with many such acoutrements of elegance, they ended up as scrap for the Second World War effort. From these buildings, general election results have been announced over the years for the St Ives constituency, which includes the Isles of Scilly. MPs who've been cheered on their election have included Captain Alec Beechman, Commander Greville Howard and Sir John Knott. The word Penzance — Pen sans — means Holy Head. The town was pillaged by the Spanish in the sixteenth century after they'd burned Mousehole and Newlyn. During the Civil War, Penzance remained loyal to the King, but residents were to pay dearly for this affiliation when Cromwell and his soldiers moved in and pillaged it again.

ABOVE *It was to Newlyn that Frank Bramley, seen here in full artistic flow, came in 1884. Like all his friends, who included Stanhope Forbes, Chevalier Taylor and Fred Hall, Bramley loved to paint in the countryside, in the street, anywhere he could observe everyday life. Bramley certainly looks the part of the artist, as he theatrically applies paint to his broad canvas. He'll perhaps be best remembered for his stunning work 'Hopeless Dawn', which he painted in 1888.*

It was an adventurous traveller indeed who ventured all the way to Cornwall in the early nineteenth century. Even with the introduction of the railway from London to Penzance in 1876, it meant a journey of nearly ten and a half hours to arrive at the country's southern tip. But many artists, inspired by Turner's earlier visits, with his sketches of St Michael's Mount, St Ives and Tintagel, decided Cornwall had to be part of their artistic education. So they headed for places like St Ives and Newlyn. A group of young artists, strongly influenced by the French painter Bastien Lepage, set up a little enclave at Newlyn. They were thrilled by the unspoilt freshness of the village. Here was the perfect place to practise the outdoor style developed by their hero Lepage.

ABOVE The imposing figure of Aunt Mary, the Bolitho family's maiden aunt. By all accounts, Aunt Mary was a sweet old dear, who took great pleasure in riding round the grounds of this country house near Penzance in a pony-driven trap. She lived at Poltair, and her brother, Thomas Robins-Bolitho, owned Trengwainton, until it passed into the hands of Sir Edward Bolitho. The origins of the house are Tudor, but it was extensively added to and changed in 1860. Miss Mary, aged about fifty here in around 1895, seems very much in command of her pony, as she sits upright, dressed in the black taffeta so popular at the time. Trengwainton gardens are now in the hands of The National Trust, and are a joy to behold all year round.

ABOVE The smell of fish can never have been far from the nostrils of people in places like Newlyn — especially the women's — for it was their job to count, clean and pack them. They were called jowsters, and here they're loading up baskets of fish which have been dumped on the beach by horse and cart from one of the fishing boats. The photograph can be dated as post-1895, as Newlyn Art Gallery can be clearly seen in the left of the background.

RIGHT The sturdy figure of the fish wife, trudging through cobbled streets, was a familiar sight up until the middle of the 1920s. With their stout boots, their gleaming white apron, and wicker cowl, or fish basket slung on their backs and held in place by a broad band on their hat, they'd sell the freshest fish available to local housewives. The fish wife was a strong, proud breed of woman, and often used to dress very smartly beneath her working costume. Business was thankfully brisk for most of the year. This woman's customer at Newlyn has her plate ready to buy fish for the evening meal.

A rare set of picture postcards, which leave nothing to the
imagination! One can be pretty sure that this group of passengers,
on a day trip from Penzance to Scilly, will not be making the same
journey again in a hurry. The rough seas, seen swelling in the first
postcard, do not augur well for the rest of the voyage, and things
can only get worse. From then on, appearances go by the board,
and it's all hands to the rails of the ship as lurching stomachs
move in time with the waves. Not a good advertisement for the
shipping company!

BELOW Pause for reflection, as a group of Victorian photographers survey the beauty of Land's End. Most famous amongst them was Herbert Hughes, a mining engineer from the colleries. In his spare time he used to tour Cornwall, with his friend and fellow camera enthusiast J. C. Burrow. They embarked on their first tour in 1897, and came back nearly every year until the start of the First World War. It's thanks to people like these that the history of this period in Cornwall is so well documented.

ABOVE The First and Last House in England, it stands on a two hundred and seventy million year-old granite site, known to the Romans as Belerion, the seat of the storms. Perkin Warbeck landed here in 1497, accompanied by six thousand Cornishmen, on an unsuccessful mission to dethrone the English king. Land's End was the haunt of smugglers, pirates and looters — a dangerous place for travellers by both land and sea. But many famous people did come here; John Wesley came twice, and wrote how appalled he was by the poverty with which the Cornish were afflicted. Turner stayed in Helston during the Napolenic War, and was moved to paint the scenic beauty of Land's End. With the arrival of the railway in 1859, the place became accessible to everyone, ending thousands of years of Celtic isolation. Now Land's End is better known as the starting or finishing post for sponsored walks, with three people arriving or leaving every week.

LEFT *Early transport in the village of Sennen, famous for its spectacular cove. Sennen, as Arthur Mee put it, is 'next door to Land's End, England's farthest west and nearest point to America'. The First and Last Inn here is one of Cornwall's best-known pubs; it's the white building nestling close to the parish church.*

BELOW The Old Success Inn at Sennen Cove. In the immortal words of Dr Samuel Johnson, 'There is nothing which has yet been contrived by man by which so much happiness is produced as by a good tavern or inn.' I doubt if he'd have found many to disagree with him then, (except those God-fearing people who signed the pledge of abstinence), and few would probably disagree with him now. Pubs like this one have fortunately escaped the ubiquitous space invaders and piped music, and still give the flavour of Old Cornwall.

ABOVE The pretty little village of Porthgwarra, just round the coast from Land's End. Its name is linked romantically with that of nearby St Leven, in the story of Sweet William and Fair Nancy. Nancy's father was a rich farmer, and in his opinion William just wasn't good enough for his daughter, so he tried to stop them seeing each other. But the lovers met secretly, and promised each other that one day they would wed. William was shortly called back to sea, and months went by without a word from him. Nancy was true to her word, however, and shunned all other suitors. She spent hours gazing out to sea at Hella Point, near St Leven, and this became known as Nancy's garden. But as time went by, and still no word from William, Nancy began to go slowly mad. Then one evening, she thought she heard him tapping at her window, beckoning her to join him at sea. She rushed to the nearby Porthgwarra Cove — later called Sweetheart's Cove, and was never seen again. What is even stranger, is that William appeared to his father the same night, telling him he'd come back for his bride, and bidding him farewell. The next day, news came of William's death, by drowning, thousands of miles away.

ABOVE A majestic view of the stately, slow-moving Helford River, once the favourite breeding ground of the otter. Taken around 1910, Sir Arthur Vivian's pleasure boat can be clearly seen on a jaunt up-river. Sir Arthur, who lived at Bosahan, was Lord Swansea's brother. His fortune came from coal, and he kept links with Wales by employing only Welsh servants in his grand house. He died about 1926. Sir Arthur was wont to partake of a drink at the Shipwright's public house, which is still thriving, but all the land behind it has now been extensively built upon. As has all the other side of the river, where the Duchy oyster beds at Port Navas have recently been blighted by disease.

BELOW The tiny village of Porthallow, near St Keverne. This photograph, taken about 1895, shows the charming thatched cottages down by the beach, where fishing boats have been rolled up, in the traditional way, on logs. A favourite fisherman's haunt was the Five Pilchards Pub, still doing good business today. The school on the hill, then recently built, is now used by the Outward Bound scheme.

ABOVE One of the greatest pleasures in compiling a book of this nature is meeting people whose memories are as fresh about events which happened at the turn of the century, as if they were last week's happenings. One of these people is Mildred Gape, a sprightly lady in her eighties, whose sparkling, mischievous eyes and bright smile are a joy to behold. She speaks enthusiastically about her youth in the pretty village of Manaccan, and here she is as a tiny tot, with her friend, in front of Forge Cottage, dressed in spotless white frock and boots. Opposite is Dagworth house, where the schoolmaster of St Martin's lived. The village school, seen behind the house, is still thriving, although numbers are sadly beginning to dwindle.

LEFT The horse bus at Manaccan about 1913. Harry Ninnes, Mildred Gape's brother, is standing up top to have his picture taken. There were two services in the village; one from the top of the village, the other from the bottom. They ran on Wednesdays and Saturdays, and competition was fierce. In fact, the two bus drivers were sworn enemies, as they were both plying for the same trade on the same days. Their horses — Hector and Polly — didn't seem to share their animosity! A typically steep Cornish village such as Manaccan needed willing folk to help the horsebus along at certain points in the journey. So on the way to Helston, any children on the bus were expected to get out at Rosevear Hill and walk to the top. Similarly, on the way back, they'd get out at St Martin's Bridge for the final push home.

BELOW Woodbine Cottage at Manaccan. Nothing is known of this particular family relaxing in their sheltered garden, on a warm summer's day. But not much has changed since this idyllic group was taken in the 1890s. Mrs Susanne Carter, who was born in this very cottage some fifty years ago, has some happy memories of this place. So much so that she built her house 'Full Circle' at the back of the property, and lives there to this day. The roses still bloom at the front of Woodbine Cottage, and the palm tree is surviving well, despite the winter gales of 1987.

ABOVE Another lucky find here. We know — from a reliable source — that it's Ernie Gossentle posting this letter at Manaccan post office around 1912. Oscar Lovesay is the boy leaning on the rail in the middle of the other boys, who are Alfie and Charlie Francis. Oscar's father was landlord of the New Inn in the village. Mary Osborne, daughter of the shopkeeper, is standing in the doorway. The family left the village in 1918, and set up shop in Peverell, Plymouth. The rail against which countless children have leant, was great for acrobatics, much to the anxiety of many a mother in the village. A wall was later built to replace it, but if you look carefully, you can still see bits of this old rail embedded in it.

BELOW Looking down on the harbour of Coverack earlier this century, one of the well-known harbours on the Lizard peninsula.

ABOVE Two postcard views of the Lizard, this time the lovely little village of Cadgwith. Here two young children enjoy the summer sunshine in the lane that slopes down to the cove (below). The whole scene has a freshness and innocence — something which seems hard to recapture. These children certainly aren't worried about passing motor cars. They'd be lucky to see even a horse and cart.

LEFT Two famous ladies, side by side: The *Cutty Sark* and the *Foudroyant,* moored in Falmouth harbour. The *Foudroyant,* the oldest ship now afloat in the Royal Navy, was a 36 gun frigate, captured at the Battle of Trafalgar. Now demasted, she sits in Portsmouth harbour, as a training ship for sea cadets. The *Cutty Sark* was, of course, the most famous of all the tea clippers used by the East India Company in the 1880s. She covered thousands of miles in her journeys from Liverpool to Ceylon, clocking up the fastest times, and making millions for her owners.

ABOVE The Prince of Wales — later King George V — lays the
foundation stone of the Prince of Wales Pier at Falmouth in 1903.
Equally interesting is what's going on in the background. For just
as one historical event is being recorded on land, another is being
recorded at sea. All the magnificence of the British fleet is
displayed here in the Men O' War. Within ten years of this
photograph being taken, the age of sail would have disappeared
forever, in terms of warships. From then on, the Iron Clads would
come into their own. They would be the forerunners of what was
to become the modern frigate and destroyer.

ABOVE Before the town of Falmouth really grew, there was a
small hamlet called Smithick, which is where the Prince of Wales
Pier now stands. It consisted of simple fishermen's huts. This
photograph shows Smithick Hill, with its corner shop. The houses
had no gardens, so all the washing was hung out to dry on poles,
suspended from the living room window. There was probably the
same rivalry to get the whitest wash to impress the neighbours, as
there still is in smaller communities today. Falmouth expanded
during the Civil War, and it was fiercely Royalist, being the last
place to give up to the Roundheads in 1646. So a garrison which
grew at the top of Smithick Hill was left to quell any residual
unrest. These simple houses, and the school on the right, have
long been demolished.

BELOW Invalid's Walk, on Falmouth's sea front, in 1906. A fashionable place to see and be seen, where nannies pushed out babies in their heavy perambulators, and where gentlemen took their constitutional. A crisp, bright, but chilly morning: the little girl on the bench, well-wrapped up in her muffler, shields her eyes against the winter sun, while the couple on the right peruse a local guide book. The now-continuous stretch of road along the town's sea front was constructed on an ad hoc basis. This last section, between Falmouth Hotel and what was then its private beach, was opened in 1908 by the Rt Honourable Haldene, Secretary of State for War. In the background are the red-brick coastguard houses, and beyond are the dwellings constructed in the early twentieth century for the soldiers of the castle garrison, now occupied by the present Falmouth coastguards. The tower on the skyline is a water tower, built for the use of the tented militia camps on the Hornworks, north of Pendennis Castle.

LEFT What better place to cut a dash when you're trying to get God's message across, than at the Seamen's Mission, at Lower Quay Hill, Falmouth? This worthy institution was part of the work of the British and Foreign Sailors' Society for the Welfare of sailors visiting the port. The Falmouth branch was founded in 1849. Visits to the ships in the harbour were made by three mission boats — *Clareen, Gift* and *Three Sisters.* Holding forth in this picture to a no-doubt enthralled congregation, is the Chaplain, Mr Roscorla. Not many preachers could boast such a pulpit, nor such a fine set of organ pipes, which are the 'bow' of the 'vessel'. As decoration in this fine chapel — the ubiquitous Victorian favourite, the aspidistra.

ABOVE The Glasgow steamer *Strathlyon* was carrying a cargo of 'fusil oil, potato meal, palm oil, sugar and toys' when she developed a leak off the Lizard. Her pumps became clogged, and it was clear she was in serious trouble. She docked in Falmouth for examination the day before this photograph was taken, and while she was being surveyed, a large explosion blew her hatch off, and a serious fire started raging. It took the local coastguard, seventy soldiers from the castle garrison, the town fire brigade and sailors from a naval vessel in the harbour, three hours to control the blaze. The damage was extensive.

ABOVE Falmouth shows off the spoils of war. There was so much 'junk' left after the First World War, it was carted round the country in a mood of feverish patriotism, as well-deserved booty. This tank, probably pushed onto the Moor in the centre of the town, was a salutary reminder of the conflict which cost so many young and promising men their lives. But the children were to know nothing of all this. For them, these were marvellous playtoys, to clamber over and explore. In this photograph, everybody wants to get in on the 'We've beaten the Bosch' bandwagon, young and old alike.

RIGHT *This picture is really rare, because it was forbidden to photograph such things during wartime. Perhaps it was taken by a naval photographer. Note the conning towers are screened, to prevent German spies taking a closer look, and recognising what type of submarine it was.*

And it wasn't just tanks that ended up in Falmouth. Four German submarines came to their end on the rocks beneath Pendennis Castle, and were to become a very popular playground for local youngsters. They are in fact still in evidence today on the castle beach, but you have to have sharp eyes to see their remains, as they're almost covered by sand. Other war relics were broken up and used as scrap in the Second World War. Sadly, that seems to have been the fate of many of the elegant railings round town houses at the time. For just as Italian women rushed out with their wedding rings and jewellery to help Mussolini and the Fascist cause, so patriotic Britishers rounded up all the scrap iron they could in the race to make more weapons of war.

BELOW First World War submarines in Falmouth Docks. The town was a defended port during the War, with a boom, or iron net across the bay, with a gate manned by ships. It stretched from St Anthony to the south of the Helford River. And it was mined. Fortunately, there wasn't much danger of air attack at the time, and the coastal guns at Pendennis Point and St Anthony rarely fired a shot in anger. The port was however a vital place to repair damaged ships which had fallen foul of the German 'U' Boats.

RIGHT All aboard who's coming aboard! A ticket collector checks to see if any more passengers want to ride the King Harry Ferry, to the east side of Falmouth Haven, at Roseland. The engine house on the left takes the great wheel, which pulls the ferry across the river, by means of heavy chains. It was said that Henry VIII came to St Mawes to oversee the building of the castle there, and that he spent the second of his six honeymoons in Roseland. And even — perhaps just a little fancifully — that he swam across King Harry Passage with Ann Boleyn on his back! So it's possible the ferry was named after the larger-than-life king. But it's more likely that it takes its name from the less controversial, and rather more gentle, Henry VI, who met his end in the Tower of London during the Wars of the Roses.

LEFT The *New Resolute,* one of several steamers which ran from
Falmouth to Truro as pleasure boats in the inter-war period. Here,
she's seen steaming south from Truro, on the high tide, passing
Trennick Row, which is just outside Truro on the Malpas road.
What's amusing about this photograph is the gaffer to the left. She
probably couldn't get away under her own wind power, so she's
taking advantage of the new technology and hitching a lift.

ABOVE One of the great social events in the farmer's calendar in
the South West: The Bath and West Show, held in Truro in 1913.
The whole town obviously entered into the spirit of the event,
with flags and bunting out in profusion in the town's Boscawen
Street. The show used to move up and down the region, changing
its venue each year, but it now has a permanent home in
Somerset.

RIGHT *An early tourist visit to
the china clay works near
St Austell.*

RIGHT *A village somewhere near St Austell in the late 1880s, a photograph taken from a glass plate. It's a touching scene of sisterly togetherness, as the little tot's uncertain steps on the cobbled streets are guided by her older sister. Her lace bonnet and pinafore are really charming. Behind them, a matronly figure, dressed in a long white apron and heavy shawl clasped around her, moves slowly down the cool, dark street.*

LEFT *Mevagissey in the 1900s – always a busy harbour and well known for producing the fastest luggers to outstrip the Preventive Men in smuggling days.*

LEFT It's easy to imagine how many proud Edwardian mothers would have been watching their darling sons in this wheelbarrow race at St Austell. The venue is long-forgotten; it was probably a school sports' day, judging from the boys' caps. Perhaps they were taking on the village team. The photograph has all the charm of a summer's afternoon in the early 1900s; it was developed from a glass slide, destined for the dustbin.

BELOW A warm summer's day, somewhere near St Austell in the 1890s, and a party of ladies and young children, all dressed in their finery, make their way down a country lane, to church, or a Sunday school outing, perhaps. The little boy in the foreground seems less willing than his two sisters to get there. All the ladies carry brollies; it was of course de rigeur to keep one's complexion pale. Rain or shine, up went the brolly or parasol. How fashions have changed!

ABOVE The main street of the old town of Bodmin, the starting
place for many a Victorian traveller, as it's only twelve miles from
the north and south coasts. It was Cornwall's principal town
before the Norman Conquest, and became a free borough in 1562.
Bodmin figured largely in the Civil War, and the Cornish Royalists
had their headquarters here for a while. The town housed the
county jail, the county police force, and the assizes. During the
First World War, Bodmin was considered a safer place than the
Tower of London for custody of the Crown Jewels.

RIGHT Part of the family of nine children who lived in
Lanhydrock house: Elverilda is near top left, with Gerald below
her and their mother Lady Clifden is sitting on the far left of the
steps. Lord Robartes took the title of Viscount of Clifden in 1899.
He's the one in the large top hat; it seems to be a favourite of his,
as many of the family photographs show him sporting it. They
were a very close family, and one that was to know much tragedy.
Two of the sons died in the First World War, and one committed
suicide after being terribly disfigured in the same war.

LEFT *Thomas C. Agar-Robartes, third from the left, and heir to Lanhydrock House, shows he's also master of the polo field. He cuts a fine dash with his three friends, as they pose as members of the Oxford University team. A life of such promise was before this young man, but it was to end tragically in 1915, when he died rescuing a comrade at the Battle of Loos. He would have inherited a marvellous house, and thanks to The National Trust, we can clearly imagine what it was like in T.C.'s day. For all the sporting paraphernalia is still laid out, as are the photographs from the family albums, the dogs' leads on the hall table, and Lady Robartes's study just as if she'd never left it. A large, elegant house, it nevertheless gives you the feeling that people really lived here — and enjoyed living here.*

ABOVE The Bathpool Band of Hope pose for a formal photograph, some time after their formation in 1902. And not a smile in sight. For saving souls was a serious business, and not a drop of alcohol had ever passed their lips. The Temperance movement was initiated by the Non-Conformist churches, especially the Methodists, in the 1800s. And the idea caught the public imagination. By setting up a Band of Hope, where all members would sign a pledge never to touch the evil drink, the group were united against a common enemy. It was a form of social outreach, which encompassed young and old. It was an excuse for meetings, for tea parties, for picnics, for singing hymns and praising the Lord. There were gaily-decorated certificates for all who signed the pledge, and by 1901, in the Weslyan movement alone, there were 427,000 members. The Bands of Hope remained popular until the 1930s. There are still some in existence in Cornwall; the one in Pelynt still meets regularly, but they're no longer a prominent force in Non-Conformist life. Attitudes towards alcohol have, of course, become less strict, although it's still not permitted to have alcohol on Methodist premises.

RIGHTTimes were different in 1904, one year after this postcard of the Latchley Band of Hope was sent to a Mr Neal, at Stoke Climsland. The Methodists thought that Balfour's Licensing Act was far too lenient, and in 1908, they tried to get a tougher bill through Parliament. But even 600,000 signatures didn't sway the Government, and it was kicked out by the House of Lords. During World War One, however, the Methodists and other such churches found the wind of change blowing their way. Excess drinking was becoming a national problem, and the Non-

Conformists found an ally in Lloyd George and the Liberal Party. The Prime Minister is quoted as saying: 'We are fighting Germany, Austria and drink. As far as I can see, the greatest of these deadly foes is drink.' Even King George V was said to have abstained for the duration of the War, so great was the public feeling against an enemy which many felt could have lost them the Conflict.

RIGHT Without question, one of the most influential and stirring figures of Cornwall's great history is the Methodist preacher John Wesley. He was just over forty when he came to Cornwall on a mission to spread the scriptures throughout this highly individualistic land. The Cornish were used to such errands; they received the message Wesley had to bring with the same enthusiasm. The Methodists first arrived in Cornwall in 1743, when a Methodist sea captain, visiting St Ives, sent out two lay preachers to spread the word. So St Ives was to become the first Methodist town, and was joined by thirty others by 1750. The weekly meetings of these fervent people took place in very simple surroundings; usually in a farmhouse kitchen, or an old out-building. They were known as 'house churches'. It was only later that prayers were said in vestries and chapels. These chapels were built with tremendous hard work and initiative, for it was obviously a costly operation, and ways and means had to be found to get the money and materials needed. One has to admire men like George Coad, a letter carrier from Saltash, who collected stones on the Devon side of the Tamar, and brought them over to Cornwall by ferry, in baskets, to build his chapel! The women weren't to be outdone either; they collected tons of sand and stone from local beaches to help the cause. Soon chapels were springing up all over Cornwall, with attendances rising all the time. Sunday schools were opened, like the one in Liskeard in 1803, whose purpose was 'to teach them to read, to teach them the principles of religion and pray with and for them, and to labour and train them for heaven'.

ABOVE *One of the charming touches of the Methodist Sunday schools, was to send out birthday cards for children in their area. Called the Cradle Roll, this card is to celebrate little Audrey Curtis's second birthday, with greetings from the Superintendent of the Cradle Roll of Liskeard Wesleyan Sunday School.*

LEFT *The imposing figure of Albert Cruse, in stately pose as he drives Alfred Truscott's hearse around 1910, in Rilla Mill. The plume holder can be clearly seen on the horse on the left, but there's none fitted to his harness here as there's nobody inside the hearse. That doesn't stop the locals coming out to have a look at who's bound on their last journey in this life!*

BELOW 'Short back and sides, please.' A miner has a trim to look his best for the Royal visit to the Phoenix Mine on 10 June 1909. Most of the large mines employed the services of a barber, and miners paid two to three pence a week out of their wages for a regular hair cut.

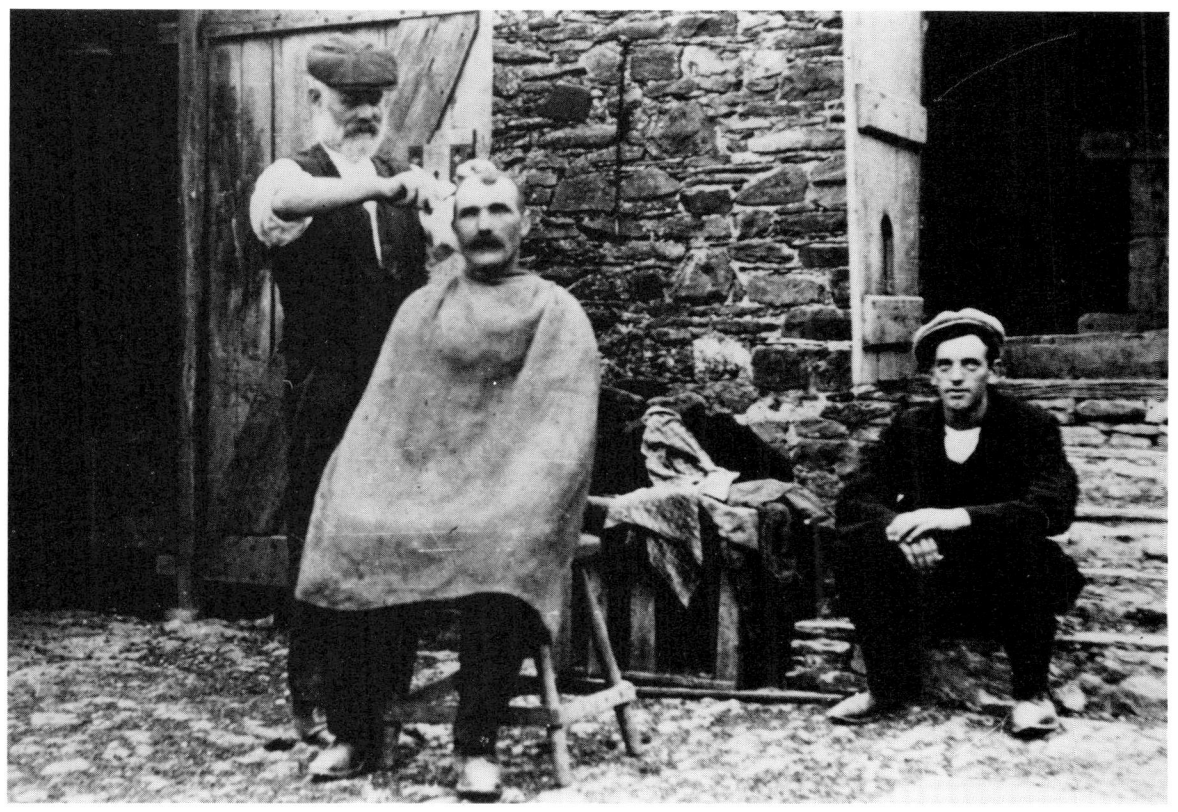

LEFT O Yea! Pensilva's crier comes out into the street to ring his bell and pass on some local news to a captive audience. Peter Skewes, the impressive man bearing the tidings, was a familiar and much-loved character in the village. With his long, white beard, and a terrier dog at his side, (the dog must have been asleep for this postcard!), he was often to be seen chatting to his neighbours, and was a mine of information. For what he missed with his eyes, he made up for with his sharp hearing. Mr Skewes was blinded in a tragic accident at Caradon Mine. He was the proud father of seven children, and his great-grandson Harry still lives in the village.

Harvesting the hay is obviously the busiest time of the year for a farmer, but this group of workers are not too busy to pose for the camera — and for posterity. For here we see some pretty sophisticated equipment for the time — 1909 — which must have made the men's lives that bit easier. Two horses are used in operating a 'sweep', which collected hay and was then pulled up by a lever to the side of the hay rick. A hay pole was erected by the side of the rick, and a gib arrangement, known as the 'gaff' would pull the hay from the ground, while the horse pulled on a wire rope, lifting it onto the rick. Sounds primitive now, compared with modern farming methods, but when everthing was previously done by hand, it was revolutionary. Ricks stood about twenty feet high in the fields. Jim Philp, the third in from the left, was the owner of this farm at Hall Barton, near Pelynt. He was a champion cider-maker, and men came from all around to taste his brew, which he served from a dipper, or ladle. Jack Ede, the man on the right, used to rent the famous Jubilee Inn in the village.

And at around five o'clock, when the men were getting tired after a long day's work in the hot sun, the women would come, bearing kettles of tea, pasties and saffron cakes. And for the uninitiated, who believe all pasties are made with meat, take note of this tourist postcard, which should put you right:

Tucking the seine at Looe. Mackerel seine boats were about thirty feet long, with a six foot beam. They had an encircling net of a quarter of a mile long, and some sixty feet deep. This is why incredible numbers of fish – sometimes in the millions – were often caught. The top of the net, or head rope, was corked to float it on the surface of the water, while at the bottom, the foot rope was leaded to weigh the net down. The seine was kept in the aft part of the boat in front of the helmsman, and the foot rope was on the foreside. The boat was rowed by a crew of six, with one other man standing in front of the piled net. His job was to shoot the net foot rope into the water at the right moment. The helmsman had to shoot the head rope and steer the boat to encircle the mackerel. Team work was the key to a successful operation. As the boat moved on the whole net, all except for the head rope, was sinking down to form a wall of net around the unsuspecting fish. The seine netting season was a summer occupation. Quite often, the mackerel would come so close to shore, they could be spotted by sharp-eyed locals, who would shout "mackerel's up" to warn the fishermen. Or specially-trained men – known as huers – would stand on the cliff tops and scour the waters below for approaching shoals. When they were in sight, the men would wave a coat or a cloth in the air to signal their approach. Another boat followed the main seiner. Its job was to drop an anchor to moor the large boat when the net was being hauled on board. This was known as tucking the seine, as seen in this photo. In the background, another seiner waits to shoot her net. The smaller boat was also used to dip fish out from the net and carry them back to market for sale. Here, the voyler, or follower, is alongside the seine boat *Dizzy*. Its baskets are ready and waiting to pull up the fish.

BELOW LEFT Taken on the eastern slip in 1880, these two women are busy cleaning pilchards for the winter. They will then take them away in the earthernware jars by their feet, to salt them back. Money and meat were scarce in winter, so families had to rely on fish as their staple diet. The pilchards were cooked with potatoes, in the brine, and were a healthy meal, as they contain an anti-coagulant. So not many fishing families suffered from heart disease.

LEFT & BELOW Looe luggers — so-called because of the cut of their sail — in harbour around 1910. The boat crews used long oars to propel themselves out through the harbour entrance, which was difficult to negotiate on certain tides. They could then row for miles out to sea, when the winds didn't oblige them, in search of their livelihood: fish. The Looe luggers, perhaps more than any other boat of their kind, cut a most impressive figure against a morning skyline.

ALSO AVAILABLE:

AROUND ST AUSTELL BAY
by Joy Wilson
An exploration in words and old photographs around one of the most beautiful bays in Britain.
'... Joy Wilson's text is as warm and as sympathetic as the lovely old pictures, making this a book which glows with interest, a soft lamplight shedding illumination on an era dimmed by the passing years. It is a beautiful achievement...'
The Western Morning News

GREAT HOUSES OF CORNWALL
by Jean Stubbs
The well-known novelist tours seven National Trust properties.
'... she finds a rich vein of history and human interest...'
The Cornish Guardian

100 YEARS AROUND THE LIZARD
by Jean Stubbs
A beautiful title, relating to a magical region of Cornwall, well illustrated, with text by the distinguished novelist living near Helston.
'... the true flavour of life on the windswept peninsula, past and present ... the strange qualities of the flat landscape, the effects of the elements on people's daily lives and, above all, the contrast of past and present are distilled in the text.'
Cornish Life

SEA STORIES OF CORNWALL
by Ken Duxbury, 48 photographs
'This is a tapestry of true tales', writes the author, 'by no means all of them disasters – which portray something of the spirit, the humour, the tragedy, and the enchantment, that is the lot of we who know the sea.'
'... a good mixture of stories, well told by a man with a close affinity to the sea and ships.'
Geoffrey Underwood
Western Evening Herald

FOWEY – RIVER AND TOWN
by Sarah Foot
An enlarged and updated edition of Following the River Fowey.
'The intricate tapestries of this delightful area is woven together with warm, understanding interviews... buy, beg or borrow it.'
The Cornish Times

DAPHNE du MAURIER COUNTRY
by Martyn Shallcross
A very special look at Cornwall in that the internationally-famous novelist has set important stories here. Explores locations which fired Dame Daphne's imagination. The subject of a Radio Cornwall series, produced by Tamsin Mitchell.
'... Anyone whose appreciation of the beauty of Cornwall has been enhanced by Dame Daphne's writing will enjoy this book – a fitting tribute to a remarkable lady.'
Cornish Life

MY CORNWALL
A personal vision of Cornwall by eleven writers who lived and worked in the county: Daphne du Maurier, Ronald Duncan, James Turner, Angela du Maurier, Jack Clemo, Denys Val Baker, Colin Wilson, C. C. Vyvyan, Arthur Caddick, Michael Williams and Derek Tangye with reproductions of paintings by Margo Maeckelberghe.
'An ambitious collection of chapters.'
The Times, London

FESTIVALS OF CORNWALL
by Douglas Williams
Douglas Williams explores some of the great Cornish occasions in the calendar: Hurling and Gorsedd, Crying the Neck and Marhamchurch Revel, Flora Day at Helston and Obby Oss at Padstow are only some of the events covered in words and photographs.
'Douglas Williams has come up trumps again ... captures the individual character of the county's festivals through his love of Cornwall and all things Cornish.'
The Cornishman

UNKNOWN CORNWALL
by Michael Williams
84 drawings and photographs nearly all especially commissioned for this publication, portraying features of Cornwall rarely seen on the published page.
'... a treasure chest of rich jewels that will surprise many people who pride themselves on a thorough knowledge ...'
Western Evening Herald

WESTCOUNTRY MYSTERIES
introduced by Colin Wilson
A team of authors probe mysterious happenings in Somerset, Devon and Cornwall.
Drawings and photographs all add to the mysterious content.
'A team of authors have joined forces to re-examine and probe various yarns from the puzzling to the tragic.'
James Belsey, Bristol Evening Post

E. V. THOMPSON'S WESTCOUNTRY
This is a memorable journey: a combination of colour and black-and-white photography. Bristol to Land's End happens to be the Bossiney region, and this is precisely E. V. Thompson's Westcountry.
'Stunning photographs and fascinating facts make this an ideal book for South West tourists and residents alike ...'
Jane Leigh, Express & Echo

COASTLINE OF CORNWALL
by Ken Duxbury
Ken Duxbury has spent thirty years sailing the seas of Cornwall, walking its clifftops, exploring its caves and beaches, using its harbours and creeks. Over 100 photographs, 45 in colour.
'... a trip in words and pictures from Hawker's Morwenstow in the north, round Land's End and the Lizard to the gentle slopes of Mount Edgcumbe country park.'
The Western Morning News

WEST CORNWALL IN THE OLD DAYS
by Douglas Williams
St Ives, Mousehole, Newlyn, Penzance, St Just, Helston and Mullion are only some of the places featured in this nostalgic book. Richly illustrated.
'... thoroughly delightful volume, packed with a splendid selection of photographs that span the mid-nineteenth century to the present day ...'
Dr James Whetter, The Cornish Banner

We shall be pleased to send you our catalogue giving full details of our growing list of titles for Devon, Cornwall, Somerset and Dorset as well as forthcoming publications. If you have difficulty in obtaining our titles, write direct to Bossiney Books, Land's End, St Teath, Bodmin, Cornwall.